BERNARD SMITH

Level 3

Series Editors: Andy Hopkins and Jocelyn Potter

Pearson Education Limited
Edinburgh Gate, Harlow,
Essex CM20 2JE, England
and Associated Companies throughout the world.

ISBN-13: 978-0-582-42737-2
ISBN-10: 0-582-42737-1

This edition first published 2000

7 9 10 8

Copyright © Penguin Books Ltd 2000
Illustrations by Nick Harris
Cover design by Bender Richardson White

Typeset by Pantek Arts Ltd, Maidstone, Kent
Set in 11/14pt Bembo
Printed in China
SWTC/07

Published by Pearson Education Limited in association with
Penguin Books Ltd, both companies being subsidiaries of Pearson Plc

For a complete list of titles available in the Penguin Readers series, please write to your local
Pearson Education office or to: Penguin Readers Marketing Department,
Pearson Education, Edinburgh Gate, Harlow, Essex CM20 2JE.

Contents

Introduction

The people in the village told me what they knew. Their stories were all true. Every word. My uncle, his wife, Rodrigo the shopkeeper – nobody lied to me. Nobody. Not even poor Clara, Rafael's mother. And she was already dead when I went back to the village. Their stories were all true. But they didn't know what really happened.

Rafael is a poor, crazy man who lives in an old boat-house on the beach in a small fishing village. What happened to him all those years ago? One day Rafael was well; the next day he was completely mad.

The writer is a doctor. He tries to find out what happened to Rafael. What made him mad? What happened to the beautiful Anita, the girl that he loved? What happened to the soldier, the stranger who came to the village? The people of the village all try to help. They tell the doctor everything they know. But only Rafael knows what really happened that night. And Rafael is mad.

Bernard Smith and his wife, Christine, teach adult foreign students in their own home near Eastbourne. Bernard has written a lot of books. Most of these are teaching books for the Arab World. He has also written about 100 examinations for Oxford-ARELS.

Other readers by Bernard Smith are *The Last Photo* and *The Man from Nowhere*.

Chapter 1   The Madman on the Beach

When I saw Rafael for the first time, I was twelve years old.

My family lived in a big town, far away from the sea. But my Uncle Miguel and his family lived in a little village on the coast. He had a café and a small farm there, and sometimes my family visited him.

There in that village I met poor, mad Rafael. I didn't know then who he was. I didn't know why he was mad. I knew nothing of his strange and terrible story. Now, fourteen years later, I know exactly what happened. But Rafael is dead. Why should I tell people his terrible secret? Only I know what happened to Rafael. Only I know what happened to the young and beautiful Anita. And to the soldier. Only I.

The people in the village told me what they knew. Their stories were all true. Every word. My uncle, his wife, Rodrigo the shopkeeper – nobody lied to me. Nobody. Not even poor Clara, Rafael's mother. And she was already dead when I went back to the village. Their stories were all true. But they didn't know what really happened.

The first time I saw Rafael, I was walking along the beach with my younger brother Pablo. Our parents were talking with my uncle and his family. We boys went along the beach to look around.

At the end of the beach there were high black rocks, where the mountains behind the village came down into the sea. Near them was an old wooden boat-house. It had no doors. The roof was broken at one end, and open to the sky. Inside there was an old wooden fishing boat.

My brother and I looked inside. The sand was deep and soft on the floor. Suddenly, in a corner behind the boat, something moved in the shadows. It was a dirty young man with long hair and a beard. He stood up and looked at us. His eyes were open, but empty. He looked at us, but he didn't see us. He was very thin.

He put one hand to his neck. I saw something shining under the dark beard. There was something small and bright on a thin fishing line round his neck. He pulled it out to show us. It was a small gold ring in the shape of a fish.

Suddenly he spoke. His voice was clear, but thin and high. He spoke words, but they didn't mean anything.

'She gave me the golden fish,' he said. 'She gave it back to me.'

Then he laughed. And when he laughed, my brother and I were very afraid. He laughed and laughed, but his eyes were big and sad. We ran out of the boat-house. The thin young man came out

behind us. He stood in the sunshine and laughed.

'She gave me the ring,' he shouted. 'I still have it.'

Some little boys from the village came running. Some of them threw stones at the thin, dirty man.

'Crazy Rafael!' they shouted. 'Crazy Rafael!'

He stopped laughing and screamed at them. Then he went back inside the boat-house. The children laughed and ran away.

We went back to my uncle's house.

'Who is that crazy man on the beach?' we asked. 'The children called him Rafael.'

'He's only a poor, mad young man,' said my uncle. 'He isn't dangerous. He went mad about a year ago. We don't know why. Nobody can help him, I'm afraid. His mother lives in the house at the end of the village. She brings him food every day. All the people in the village help her when they can.'

Soon the adults began to talk about other things. But I never forgot poor, mad Rafael. Every time I thought about the village, I remembered the poor, mad man in the boat-house on the beach. Sometimes I saw him in my dreams. He looked at me with his big, empty, mad eyes. He called to me. He had the gold ring round his neck, and he held it out to me. He called for me to help him.

♦

My family went back to the town. After I left school, I went to university in the capital. I studied to be a doctor. I spent two years in the USA. Finally, I came back to my home town and I found work in a big, new hospital there.

In all those years, I never went back to the village. But then one of my uncle's sons got married and all my family went there for a few days.

There were many changes in the village. Twelve years of change. There were new stone houses. There were new, brightly-painted fishing boats along the beach, a lot of them with engines. My uncle had a big, clean, new café with tables and chairs, and a television in the corner. It was all very different from the village that I saw as a boy.

I went down to the beach on my first afternoon in the village. I wanted to see again the place where I first saw Rafael. I couldn't believe it. The old boat-house and the boat were still there. The boat was in pieces now, but the boat-house was bigger and stronger. There was some new wood on the walls and a new roof on it.

I walked along the beach and felt the soft sand under my town shoes. There was a man sitting near the old boathouse. He was looking at the sea. He had long hair and long, thin legs. I came closer and he suddenly looked round at me. It was Rafael. I saw again those same wide, crazy, sad eyes, the eyes from my dreams.

He was twelve years older. His hair and beard were beginning to go grey, but they weren't as long and dirty as before. His face was very thin and he looked ill. His clothes were old, but clean.

'How are you, Rafael?' I called, smiling.

He put his head on one side and looked at me. His mouth opened and he smiled. A thin brown hand moved up to his neck.

'She gave me the golden fish,' he said. His voice was flat and empty. He coughed suddenly – a deep, dry cough. Then he looked with sad yellow eyes at the bright, empty sea.

I went back across the soft white sand to my uncle's house. I had an idea in my head. I was a doctor now. Perhaps I could find out what was the matter with this poor man. I could give him the best help that modern medicine could give him.

I told my uncle what I wanted to do. 'There are special hospitals now in the capital for people like Rafael. I can take him there. If I can make him well, I will. If not, he can stay in a hospital there. He will have a bed, good food, nurses all the time. It's not good for him to sleep on the beach. He looks ill.'

I asked him to tell me about Rafael. He told me everything that he knew. It was a long and strange story. I wrote it all in a notebook. I wanted to help the poor madman to get well. For this, I had to know everything about him.

Chapter 2   Rafael's Father and the Sharks

Told by my uncle

Rafael was born in the village (my uncle said).

His father was called Manuel and he was a fisherman. His mother, Clara, is also dead now. She was the sister of my own wife, Rosa. Rafael was their only child. He was a fine boy, never ill, good-looking, healthy and strong.

When he was about eight years old, his father was killed. It was a terrible thing for the young boy. He was there and saw his father die. They were out in their boat, fishing with some other men from the village. I don't know what happened exactly. Something happened to the fishing nets; perhaps they were caught under the boat. Manuel went into the water to do something with them.

Suddenly a shark attacked him. It was a complete surprise. The other fishermen could do nothing to help him. It was a big white shark. It came up from deep water and bit off one of Manuel's legs – a clean bite above the knee.

The other men pulled him into the boat. The blood from his leg ran deep in the bottom of the boat. The men put a shirt round the top of his leg. They tried to stop the blood, but it was impossible. They say that Manuel was calm at first. He felt no pain. He smoked a cigarette and he talked to little Rafael, in the boat next to him.

But after a few minutes he went very white. Then he began to feel very cold. The men covered him with their clothes to keep him warm. But he became very weak and sleepy.

Suddenly he put his hand on Rafael's head.

'Be a good son,' he said. His voice was terribly tired. 'Help your mother.' Then he fell asleep, and in a few minutes his heart stopped.

After that, Rafael and his mother, Clara, lived alone in their house at the end of the village. Manuel's brother, Ricardo, helped Clara with money. All the people in the village helped her. Manuel was a good man. We always help our people when they need it. In a few years Rafael was older and started to work. He became a fisherman too. He and his mother were poor, but he could earn enough money for them both.

Rafael was a fine boy. He became a good fisherman. But he always hated sharks, because of what happened to his father. Every few months, he did something very strange. When anyone in the village killed an animal for meat, Rafael asked them for the skin and

the stomach. He took the insides of the animal that nobody wanted. Then he went out in his boat alone, far from the land. There he threw the pieces of the animal into the sea and waited for the sharks to come. A shark can smell blood in the water when it is many kilometres away. Soon a lot of sharks arrived in the water round his boat. Then Rafael took his fishing spear. He stood up in his boat and killed one or two of them.

When he killed a shark, the other sharks tasted the blood. They began to bite and eat the shark. So then there was more blood in the water and more sharks came. Rafael killed more and more. After an hour he was almost too tired to stand. It was a really dangerous thing to do in a small boat.

But he was smiling when he told me about it. He was really happy about the dead sharks, because a shark killed his father.

So Rafael grew up, tall, strong and good-looking. And, of course, he fell in love with Anita, the shopkeeper's daughter. So now, (said my uncle) I have to tell you about Anita, too.

Chapter 3 Anita, the Shopkeeper's Daughter

Told by my uncle

Anita was a beautiful child (my uncle continued). I know, most children are beautiful. But she was the most beautiful child that I've ever seen. Everyone loved her. Little children, old people, men and women, they all loved Anita. They smiled when they saw her. And year after year she grew up, and year after year she grew more beautiful.

Her father, Rodrigo, the shopkeeper, loved her most. He tried to keep her close to him, always. She could never go out and talk with the village boys. But this is a small village. It was impossible to keep her at home all the time. She was a good girl, but all the young men dreamed of her and wanted to marry her.

She was not only beautiful. She was clever, too. Her father could read and write. Most of the people in the village couldn't. We had no school in the village in those days. So Rodrigo taught Anita to read and write. He often went into the town to buy things for his shop. Then he brought back picture magazines and small story books for her.

Anita was very good at reading and telling stories. She remembered everything that she read. When she was only nine or ten, she often sat near the house under a tree with a book. There she read or told stories to her little brothers and sisters. Soon the other children of the village came and sat round her. Some of the fishermen, old and young, sat on the beach near the shop, too. They liked to listen to little Anita when she told her stories.

Of course, Rodrigo had big plans for Anita. He was so proud of her. He wanted her to marry someone rich and important. Perhaps a man from the city, who was able to help Rodrigo's business. Everyone knew one thing for sure. He didn't want Anita to marry anyone from the village.

Rafael loved her very much. They say Anita loved him, too. But there was no hope for him. Rodrigo didn't want a poor fisherman to be Anita's husband.

Poor Rodrigo. He loved Anita and he had great hopes for her. When she ran away, it was terrible for him. He still doesn't talk about it. Not a word. Not after all these years. For him, he says, Anita is dead. He has no daughter of that name.

♦

'But where did she go?' I asked my uncle. 'Someone knows. And why is Rafael mad? Not because Anita ran away from home. She didn't run away with *him*, did she?'

'No, she didn't,' answered my uncle. 'That's for sure. Nobody knows where she went. But Rafael stayed in the village. And that was the time when he went mad. I believe that Anita ran away with the soldier. I think they're married. They're probably living in another town, far away. But that's only my opinion. I don't really know.'

'The soldier? What soldier?' I asked. My uncle smiled and looked at his watch. 'It's a long and strange story,' he said.

Chapter 4   The Soldier

Told by my uncle

The soldier (said my uncle) came to the village about three months before Anita ran away. She was sixteen years old then, and Rafael was eighteen.

The soldier was a strange man. His real name was Carlos, but everyone called him 'the soldier'. He told us about his life.

'I've been a soldier all my life,' he told us. 'I was in Cuba for six years. Then I fought in Africa and many other places. I've seen the world, my friends.'

He had a thousand stories. But nobody ever knew where he came from. He was very handsome, with bright eyes and long, dark hair. He was a soldier, a sailor, a fisherman – everything. He had a small boat with an engine. That was unusual in those days. He worked for nobody. He went where he wanted to. He did what he wanted to. He bought things and sold things. He could get anything that you wanted, for a price.

He sailed into our village late one afternoon. He anchored his boat a few metres from the shore and walked up the beach. I never knew what he came for. It was just a small thing that he wanted, probably. First he went to Rodrigo's shop. Then he came to my café and sat for an hour and talked. And there he saw Anita, sitting by the corner of the shop. The children were all round her on the ground and she was telling them a story.

He sat outside the café and talked for an hour or more about this and that. But his eyes never went far from the little group of children.

At last he asked me: 'Is that girl your schoolteacher?'

I laughed and said: 'No, she's just the shopkeeper's daughter. She's only sixteen. She's not much older than a child.'

He left the village late in the afternoon before it got dark. He walked through the water to his boat and climbed in. We watched him start the engine. The boat moved away round the rocks at the end of the beach. Everyone in the village stopped what they were doing. Anita, too, stopped in her story. Everyone watched the strange thing – a boat that went without a sail.

Of course, he came back. I told you, no man could ever forget Anita. A week or two later his boat arrived again and the good-looking stranger went to Rodrigo's shop. He bought a few things and talked with Rodrigo. Then he came to the café again. He had a drink and a talk with me. Then he went off again along the coast.

Soon he came twice a week, on Thursdays and Sundays. He made friends with the people of the village. He was exciting and amusing. He was different from the people of the village. He was a stranger, but everyone seemed to like him. We listened to the stories about his travels and his life in other countries. He always spent an hour or two at my café. He sat and drank with us and told funny stories. Many of the fishermen came to the café when he was there. I liked him, the other men did, too.

He often brought little presents for people. He brought me a little cassette player one day. It was something new for us. We had no electricity in the village then, and we knew very little about the outside world. He showed me how it worked. Then he brought me new batteries for it every two weeks. He gave me some cassettes for it, too, of music from the cities, dance music from Latin America, and Mexican love songs.

'A café must have music,' he said, 'music for the customers to enjoy.'

After that I kept the little cassette player on the bar. Every time the soldier came to the café, I played some music for him. When the café was busy, I played music for the people of the village, too.

He brought a paraffin lamp for Rodrigo to put in his shop. It was a very bright light. No house in the village had a light like it. The soldier was becoming very good friends with Rodrigo.

Then early one Monday morning, we heard a terrible noise from Rodrigo's house. He was shouting, his wife was screaming, and the children were all crying. It seems Anita wasn't in the house. Her bed was cold and empty. There was no note from her, not a word. Rodrigo wanted to get the police.

'Somebody has stolen my daughter,' he said. 'Somebody has taken her away in the night, dead or alive.'

But then they found that her little box was empty. Anita's best clothes and favourite things weren't there. Even her little story books were gone. So Rodrigo stopped talking about bringing the police. For a few days he was terribly angry. He spoke wildly and fought with everyone. Nobody could speak to him. Then, suddenly, he seemed to cut her out of his life. He never spoke her name again. He still doesn't talk about her. Only a brave man speaks Anita's name in front of him.

We never saw the soldier again. He was here on the Sunday afternoon and evening. He usually was. He spent most of the evening in the café, listening to the music. Then he left at about ten o'clock. I watched him go out to his boat. It was dark. There was no moon. But I heard him start his engine and go off to the west. And the next morning Anita was gone. And we never saw her or the soldier again.

So I – and most people in the village – believe that she ran away with the soldier. Nobody knows how they did it. We never saw him talk to her for a minute in the village. I think he waited for her in his boat along the coast. And she went to him in the middle of the night. Most of us believe they are living together somewhere. Maybe with their own children now.

♦

'But why did Rafael go mad?' I asked my uncle.

'Who knows?' he replied. 'Perhaps he went mad because he loved Anita. Then she ran away with the soldier. Who can say? He did love the girl very much. I knew it, and his mother did, too. But marriage was impossible because Rafael was a poor, fatherless fisherman.'

'But a man doesn't go mad for thirteen years because a girl runs away from home,' I said. 'Men often lose their wives, their children. People die in accidents. This doesn't make other people crazy. Rodrigo lost his favourite daughter, the light of his life, but he didn't go mad.'

'Who can say?' said my uncle again. 'Who knows why things happen? Why does a man go mad? We know that Rafael was in love with Anita. He loved her for a long time before the soldier came to the village. We know that because of the gold ring.'

'Ah, yes,' I said. 'Tell me about the gold ring that Rafael wears round his neck. It's clearly a very important part of the story.'

Chapter 5   The Gold Ring

Told by my uncle

Rafael (said my uncle) was in love with Anita. He wanted to marry Anita when she was only fifteen or sixteen. His mother went to see Rodrigo to talk to him about it. I heard that Rodrigo was very polite to her.

'I'm sorry,' he said. 'Anita is going to marry a rich businessman in the city. He's a very rich man and a friend of our family. Your son Rafael is a fine boy. But he's too young to get married. And he has nothing to give her. Nothing at all.'

Rafael was very sad when he heard about Anita and the businessman. Then, after a few weeks, he suddenly left the village and went to the port on the coast.

'I'm going to find work in the port,' he said to his mother. 'I want to see something of the world outside this village. I'll come back in a month or two.'

He put his few things in his boat and sailed along the coast to the port. It was six months before we saw him again.

◆

'Six months? What did he do there for six months?' I asked my uncle.

'You're lucky,' he replied. 'I can tell you. Rafael came to the café one evening. There were no other customers that night, and he told me about his time in the port. This is what he told me.'

◆

Rafael stayed in the port all the time (my uncle said). He slept in his boat on the beach. Sometimes he bought fruit and vegetables from the market after it closed. They were very cheap then. He worked for anyone. He did anything. He carried things for people. He loaded and unloaded boats and lorries. Every morning, very early, he went fishing. Then he sold the fish on the beach before he started work. Slowly, very slowly, he began to save some money.

Rafael met an old goldsmith in the town. He was a good old man. Rafael helped the goldsmith when he could. He cleaned his shop for him and brought packages and messages for him. He talked to him and made coffee for him. He watched him while he was working. Soon he became a good friend.

Rafael never took any money from the old man. He never asked for any.

Then, one day, the goldsmith asked Rafael what he wanted. He knew he wanted something. And Rafael told him.

'I want a gold ring for a girl in my village,' he said. 'It must be in the shape of a fish, a long fish with its tail in its mouth. How much will this ring cost? I have some money. I know it's not enough. But I'll work for you until I've paid for it.'

The old goldsmith made the ring for him. I'm sure Rafael paid much less than its real cost. But it took six months of hard work to pay for it.

Soon after Rafael came back to the village, he went with his mother to see Rodrigo. This time Rafael spoke for himself.

'Señor* Rodrigo,' he said quietly. 'My father is dead and my mother is poor. But I'm hard-working and honest and I'll be a good husband to Anita. One day I'll be a rich man, like your friend in the city. But I'll be a better husband to Anita than the businessman, because I love her with all my heart.'

Then he gave the gold ring to Rodrigo as a present for Anita.

Of course, Rodrigo didn't agree to a marriage between Anita and Rafael. He gave the ring back to Rafael.

'I'm sorry,' he said. 'But Anita will marry the businessman in a year or two. That is decided and I am not going to change my plans.'

♦

'So Anita never got the ring,' I said to my uncle. 'After all that work and time, he couldn't give it to her.'

'He still has it on a piece of fishing line round his neck,' my uncle said.

*Señor: the Spanish word for Mr.

15

'And when did the soldier come to the village for the first time?'

'A few months after Rafael came back from the port, perhaps. I can't remember exactly.'

'But Rafael wasn't mad at that time?'

'Oh, no. Not at all. In fact he seemed very happy.'

'Tell me about the time when he went mad. Was it the same time exactly when Anita went away with the soldier, or later?'

'It's difficult to remember. A lot of things happened at that time.'

'What do you mean? What kind of things happened?'

'Oh, little things, strange things. Santiago's old donkey disappeared.'

'What do you mean – it disappeared?'

'It did – it went. It disappeared. One day it was in the field behind his house. The next day it wasn't there. Perhaps Anita stole it to ride on. But everyone knew Santiago's donkey. It was too old and weak to walk a hundred metres. It couldn't carry a girl.'

'What other strange things happened?'

'I remember that on that last night, Rafael danced.'

'Danced?'

'Yes, he danced for hours, alone, here in the café. He never danced before, not in the café or anywhere. Or I never saw him dance. And, of course, he never danced again, because he went crazy. But I must start at the beginning.'

Chapter 6   The Night When Rafael Danced

Told by my uncle

It was a Sunday (said my uncle). The soldier arrived in his boat in the early afternoon, when everything was quiet. He lowered his anchor a few metres from the shore, as usual, and walked up the sand to the houses. He never pulled his boat up on to the beach. It was a heavy boat and it he didn't want to break the engine. He always left it in about one metre of water.

That day he came first to the café. He sat and talked with me and some of the men. We all sat outside the café and listened to his stories.

Then, later in the afternoon, he went to Rodrigo's shop and bought a few things. He had a big can of paraffin in the boat for Rodrigo's new lamp. I saw him give it to him. The soldier and Rodrigo sat and talked and drank coffee outside the shop for about an hour.

When it got dark, he went with Rodrigo into the house behind the shop. I could see the bright light from the lamp through the window. Then the soldier had a meal with Rodrigo.

After the meal, he came back to the café and sat with me and some of the fishermen. It was very dark and we sat inside. The soldier seemed very happy. He told us a lot of funny stories about his life as a soldier.

Then, at about nine o'clock, Rafael came into the café.

We were surprised to see him, because Rafael didn't spend a lot of time at the café. And he never came into the café when the soldier was there. That night he was wearing his best clothes. Usually he wore his old clothes, even in the café. He was wearing his best shirt and trousers. His face and hands were very clean, and his hair was still wet and shiny from washing. I asked myself: 'Is he trying to show the soldier that he is not just a poor fisherman?'

The soldier knew Rafael. He knew that he wanted to marry Anita. Everyone in the village talked about it. Rafael knew that the soldier was also interested in her. Everyone in the village talked about that, too. But nobody knew the secret game that the soldier was playing.

Rafael and the soldier didn't speak. The café was quiet. Nobody spoke.

Suddenly the soldier took a cassette from his pocket.

'Let's have some music,' he said, giving me the cassette.

I took it and put it into the player. I remember it was a love song. It was sung by a girl with a soft and beautiful voice. We all sat and listened to it. Rafael smiled and listened, too.

When the cassette ended, I put another cassette in the player. But the soldier stood up.

'It's getting late,' he said. 'I must go.'

He went out into the dark night. It was about ten o'clock, I think. His usual time. A few minutes later, we heard the noise when he started the engine of his boat. Then the sound of the engine went slowly along the coast. Soon everything was quiet again. We could hear only the sea and the music.

The girl on the cassette was singing another love song. It was a sad song, slow but strong. The fishermen and I sat quietly and listened.

Suddenly Rafael stood up in the corner of the café and began, very slowly, to dance. Alone in the shadows, his eyes closed, he moved to the music.

He danced, his head back, eyes closed, a strange half-smile on his face. We all watched him in surprise. After a few minutes we laughed and went on talking. But Rafael went on dancing, dancing alone for the rest of the evening. Every time the music stopped he looked at me with big, dark eyes and said, 'Again.' And I put another cassette in the machine. Then Rafael smiled, closed his eyes, and continued dancing.

At midnight all the other men went off to bed. Rafael was still there, still dancing. I watched the poor boy until the song ended. Then I switched off the machine. I said good night to him, and sent him home to bed.

Then the next morning, before daylight, we heard shouting and crying from

Rodrigo's house. The news went round the village like fire. Anita wasn't there.

Rodrigo sent all his family and friends out to look for her. They looked along every road, big and small. They looked in the fields and along the beach, in the rocks. Everywhere.

Later, Rafael came out of his house with his mother. I told them about Anita, and they were very surprised. We all were. Rafael went to his boat immediately. He planned to sail along the coast and look for her.

He sailed away to the west. I watched him until I couldn't see him. He sailed round the rocks at the end of the village. He was looking at the land as he went. The next time I saw him, he was mad.

Everybody in the village was out looking for Anita that morning. But nobody found her. Then Santiago couldn't find his old donkey. He came to Rodrigo's shop. He was shouting that Anita took it. Rodrigo was very angry. He wanted to hit Santiago and knock him down. I thought he wanted to kill the old man. Some friends of Santiago took him away quickly. After that, he said nothing more about the donkey.

Then, early in the afternoon, some of the fishermen found Rafael. He was about a kilometre west of the village, in a quiet place near the high rocks. His boat wasn't far from the shore and Rafael was lying in the bottom of it. He was wet and dirty. He was looking up at the sky and laughing. And he was completely mad.

They brought him and the boat back to the village. His mother and I washed him and gave him some water. We put him to bed. But he lay and made noises all night. He screamed and fought. He was like a mad animal.

The next day he went out of the house and sat by his boat. He looked at the sea all day and said nothing. We waited, day after day. We gave him food and drink. We washed him when we could. But he was like a small child. We waited for him to get better. But he never did.

♦

'And you never found out what made him mad?' I asked my uncle.

'He never speaks. Only about the ring. You know everything that I know now,' he said. 'When we were washing the poor boy, we found the gold ring on a fishing line round his neck. When we tried to take it off, he screamed. So we left it there. All these years later, he still wears it round his neck. He gave six months of his life to buy that ring. His present for Anita which she never had.'

Chapter 7   Two Visits

The next morning, I went with my uncle to see Rodrigo, the shopkeeper. He had a fine supermarket now, built of stone. He still lived in a house behind the shop. But now the house was two floors high and had a garden with a wall round it. He also had his own lorry with his name on it, and there was a new car next to the shop. It was clear that Rodrigo had plenty of money now.

Inside the supermarket there were all kinds of tins and packets. There were boxes of fresh fruit and vegetables outside the door. It was the biggest shop in the village and it seemed to sell everything.

Rodrigo was a big, heavy man. He was about fifty years old and he wore a fine white suit and a white hat. When we arrived, he was unloading boxes of tins from the lorry. He was picking them up, three at a time, and taking them into the shop. He was big and fat. But he was still a very strong man.

He was polite and friendly to my uncle and me. He knew I

was a doctor. He invited us into his house. We sat and had coffee and talked about the changes in the village since my first visit as a boy.

At last I told him my ideas for helping Rafael. Then he wasn't so friendly.

'A doctor!' he said. 'He needs more than a doctor. I don't know why he's crazy. Nobody does. God knows, I've helped him and his mother over the years. I've given them food when they were hungry. And money when they needed it. His poor mother was a good and hard-working woman. Now she's dead. It was a terrible thing to happen to her. Terrible. First her young husband was killed by a shark. Then her only son went crazy and lived on the beach like an animal.

'Some people say that love made him mad. But you're an intelligent man, doctor. You've studied at university. Does a young man of eighteen years go mad for love of a girl? A strong young man in good health? It's a stupid idea. I believe he wasn't in good health. I think he was ill. I don't know the problem exactly. You're the doctor. Help him. Make him better, if you can. But look for the facts. Don't listen to people's silly stories.'

'So you don't think that your daughter Anita was the reason for his madness?' I asked.

Rodrigo didn't look at us. He looked at the wall for a long time.

'I don't have a daughter called Anita,' he said at last. 'I had one many years ago, but she's dead.'

After that, he said nothing more about Rafael or Anita. Soon we thanked him and left.

◆

Later that morning, a man came to my uncle's house. He was small and thin. He stood at the back door with his hat in his hands.

22

When my uncle saw him, he brought him inside. He found a chair for him and gave him a drink.

'This is Luis Valdez,' he said to me. 'He's a farmer. He has a farm just outside the village to the east.'

We sat and talked about farms and the weather. Then the man began to ask me about Rafael.

'Is it true, the story that I hear?' he asked. 'Are you trying to save Rafael, the poor, crazy boy?'

'I'm a doctor,' I answered. 'And yes, I'm interested in Rafael. I'm trying to find out why he went mad. Perhaps I can make him better. Perhaps not.'

'My wife asked me to talk to you,' he said. 'She's Marta, Rodrigo's second daughter and Anita's younger sister. She says she wants to talk to you about Anita and Rafael. But it must be a secret. She knows things that even her father Rodrigo doesn't know. She wants to help Rafael. But she doesn't want to make her father angry or unhappy after all these years.'

'Her secrets will be safe with me,' I said. 'I don't want to make the people in the village unhappy. I only want to help Rafael. If she knows anything about Rafael, I'll be happy to talk to her.'

That evening I went alone to Luis's house. Luis sent his children to bed, and Marta began to tell me her story.

Chapter 8   The Young Princess

Told by Marta

I'm Rodrigo's second daughter (Marta told me). I was seven years younger than Anita. When I was a little girl, it was very strange. Anita was beautiful; I wasn't. Anita was clever; I wasn't. She could read and tell stories, sing and draw pictures. I couldn't. I was small, fat and stupid. But I've been lucky. I married a good husband. I

23

have two healthy sons and a pretty daughter. Now I'm very happy with my life.

But I must tell you about my sister Anita. It's true that she was beautiful and clever. But, I'm sorry to say, she wasn't a very good child. Not very nice. Our parents gave her everything she wanted. She could do anything she liked. She never worked or helped our mother in the house. I remember that her hands were always clean and beautiful. Her fingernails were long and pink. They were never broken or bitten like mine.

Everyone thought she was beautiful and clever. Everyone smiled at her. Everyone did what she wanted.

She became proud and lazy. I remember she told us stories, sitting near the house. But her voice was very loud and clear, and all the people near us could hear her clever words. She often sang to herself in the house. But she sang only when there were people outside to hear her.

I'm sorry. This isn't important, really. But she did other things. Worse things.

We slept in a small room at the back of the old house. I was only eight or nine years old then. Anita had most of the room for her things, and I slept in the corner.

One night, I remember, it was very late. Our parents were in their room asleep, and something woke me up. I saw Anita going quietly out of the room. She was wearing a dress and shoes. The moon was very bright that night, and I couldn't sleep again. I lay awake, waiting. About half an hour later, Anita came quietly back into the room and got into her bed.

'Where have you been?' I asked her.

She was very angry, because I was awake.

'Go to sleep, stupid girl,' she said. 'I had stomach-ache. I only went out for a few minutes. Don't say anything to anyone.'

I said nothing, but after that I watched her. I saw her go out on other nights. At last, I asked her where she went.

She laughed quietly. 'I go to meet my prince,' she said. That was all that she said. Her head was full of the stories that she read in her books. She loved stories about princes and princesses. Stories about magic carpets which could fly, and magic lamps and rings. These were the stories that she told us most often. She didn't have to read them. She knew them all. She imagined that she was a beautiful princess in a story. She never believed that she was only a shopkeeper's child. Perhaps a king gave her to her parents in secret when she was a baby. She had many strange and silly ideas in her head.

◆

'But who did she go to see? Who was this prince?' I asked Marta.

'It was Rafael, of course,' she replied. 'They were in love. Even when they were little children. She went out at night to the big rocks at the end of the beach. Rafael came and met her there. They sat there in the rocks in the moonlight. They talked about their love and the happy married life that they planned.

'Our parents had no idea that she was doing this, of course. Anita told me to keep quiet about it. "If you tell anyone," she said, "I'll say terrible things about you to our parents. They'll believe me. They won't believe you." And it was true. I knew it was true. They always believed Anita.

'She could always do what she wanted. I was always in trouble. So I said nothing.

'Then Rafael went away to work in the port. For six months, Anita lost her prince. In the daytime, she was the same as before. But at night she cried in her bed, because her Rafael was far away.

'But when he came back, she was happy again. She went to meet him at the big rocks.

'After a few days she came back from one of these meetings with a ring on her finger. She showed it to me in the moonlight in our room. It was the gold ring in the shape of a fish. She was very proud of it. She wore it on her finger when she went to meet Rafael. At other times she kept it under the carpet in our room.'

Marta stopped and drank from a glass of water. I didn't know what to say. This wasn't the same Anita that my uncle described to me.

'Do you know what happened to Anita?' I asked. 'Do you know where she went that night? The night she went away?'

Marta thought for a few long seconds.

'I can remember what I saw. And I can remember what I heard,' she said. 'I remember all that exactly. I shall never forget it. But I'm still not sure what happened.'

Chapter 9   The True Prince

Told by Marta

On that Sunday night (Marta continued), I went to bed early. About eight o'clock, I think, like most younger children. My father was in the living room. He was talking to the soldier. The soldier stayed for a meal that evening. I could hear their voices through the walls. They had the new paraffin lamp in there with them, I remember. It made a bright light in that room.

Anita was in our room, too. Father sent her to bed because the soldier was there. She was lying on her bed and reading by the light of a small oil lamp. She was listening to the talk in the living room, too. I remember that we could hear the soldier's deep voice very clearly through the thin walls.

I think I fell asleep. When I woke up, it was later, but not very late. The bright light from the lamp was still shining under the door of the living room. My parents were in there, talking quietly. But the soldier wasn't there with them.

Anita was taking things out of her box and putting them in a bag. I sat up and spoke to her.

She told me to be quiet. She continued taking her best dresses out of the box and putting them in the bag. I asked her what she was doing. 'I'm going to meet my true love, my true prince,' she said. 'I'm going away with him.' She laughed and sang quietly, 'The girl with the magic ring will always know her true love.'

She told me to say nothing. Then she went very quietly to the back door and went out into the dark night. Her hand quietly pulled the door closed behind her. On her middle finger she wore the gold ring shaped like a fish.

I went to the window and looked out. I was terribly afraid. I knew Anita was a silly child, but this was very, very wrong. 'If Father finds out, he'll kill her,' I thought. 'He gets angry very quickly, and he's very strong.' But I was afraid of Anita, too. So I stood there looking out of the window. I cried quietly.

There was no moon and it was very dark. I heard music playing in the café along the beach. It was a nice song, a slow song. I listened to the music and the soft sound of the waves on the beach. Soon I felt a little better. After a long time, I started to feel cold. So I went back to my bed and fell asleep.

I woke up again much later. The house was dark and quiet. My parents were asleep. Nobody was talking anywhere in the house. Anita's bed was still empty. I went to the window again. The moon was up and I could see the houses along the beach. There was still a light in the café and music playing.

I went back to bed. I cried until I fell asleep. I hoped that it was all a bad dream.

When I woke again, the first grey light of the new day was in the room. Anita's bed was still empty. I lay in bed with my eyes closed until my mother came to wake us. When she found Anita's empty bed, she started to shout and scream. Then I opened my eyes. I soon started to cry, too. I never told them where she went.

Or what she said. There was terrible shouting and crying in our house that day. But we never saw Anita again.

♦

'So you think she went to see Rafael that night?' I said slowly.

'Oh, no,' said Marta. 'I think she went to meet the soldier, Carlos. That's why she called him her *true* prince. He was like someone in a story, you see. First the beautiful princess falls in love with a poor fisherman. Then either he turns into a handsome prince, or a real prince comes along and takes her away to his palace. I'm afraid Anita was quite a silly girl, really. She lived the stories in her head. After the soldier came to the village, she started to meet him at night. She went to the same place in the rocks. But she was meeting the soldier, not Rafael. She went there many times. Then, that night, she didn't come back. She went away with him in his boat. In those days, perhaps, a boat with an engine was like a magic carpet.'

'But she was wearing the gold ring when she went?' I said.

'Yes, she took all her best things: dresses, her story books, and the ring.'

'But Rafael has that ring. He has worn it round his neck for more than thirteen years.'

'I know,' she said. 'I think she spoke to Rafael that night. I think she told him her plans. Then she gave him his ring and went off to meet the soldier somewhere along the coast.'

'Is that what you really think?' I asked.

'Yes,' said Marta. 'She said goodbye to Rafael and gave him his ring. Then she went to meet the soldier. That's what made Rafael mad. He went to look for her the next day, but all the time he had the ring round his neck. He wanted her to come back. Or he wanted her father to find her and bring her back. But she never came. And when she didn't come, Rafael went mad. When you talk to Rafael, what does he say?'

29

'He holds the ring, and says, "She gave me the ring," or "She gave me the golden fish",' I answered.

'Exactly,' said Marta. 'First she took his ring and said, "I love you." Then she gave it back to him and went away with the soldier. That's what made the poor man crazy.'

'What was so special about the ring?' I asked. 'What did Anita say? Something about a magic ring?'

'The girl with the magic ring will always know her true love. It was in her story,' said Marta. 'Her own story. She wrote it herself. It wasn't a story that she read in a book. It was her favourite story. She told it to us hundreds of times.'

'And it was about a magic ring?'

'Yes. In fact, I have the story here. Anita wrote it in a notebook and I kept it. It's the only thing of Anita's that I have. I can't read it, of course, but it's that story.'

Marta went into another room and came back with a small, thin notebook. She carried it carefully in both hands. She put it on the table in front of me.

It was a cheap school writing book. The pages were yellow with age. There was only one story in it. It was called 'The Ring of the Golden Fish'. The story was short. It was written in pencil in the large, clear writing of a young child.

Luis and Marta looked at me. I realized they were waiting. They wanted to hear me read the story to them.

Chapter 10   'The Ring of the Golden Fish'

This is the story that I read to Marta and her husband. The story that was written by Anita all those years ago.

A long time ago, there was a beautiful princess. She lived in a beautiful palace with big, beautiful gardens all round it. But she was sad because she had no friends. She couldn't talk to anyone or play with anyone. She was a prisoner in the palace because she was so beautiful.

Her father wanted her to marry a rich, handsome prince. But the princes in that country weren't handsome. And the rich men weren't princes. And the handsome men weren't princes or rich. So she married nobody, and she was very sad.

One day, a poor fisherman came to the beach at the end of the palace gardens. The gardens were very big and went as far as the sea. The fisherman caught a big golden fish and he wanted to kill it. But it was a magic fish and it spoke to him.

'Don't kill me,' it said, 'and I'll give you a magic ring. And with this ring you can marry the princess.'

So the handsome young fisherman put the fish back into the sea. Soon it came back with a gold ring in its mouth.

'The man with this magic ring will always know his true love,' said the fish. And it swam away to the bottom of the sea.

The handsome young fisherman was called Roberto. (Here the name Rafael was written first and then changed.) *When Roberto put on the ring, he saw in his head a picture of the princess. He fell in love with her.*

He walked through the gardens to the palace, looking for the princess. When he found her in the garden, he put the magic ring on her finger. And she knew immediately that she loved the handsome young fisherman. They went to her father, the king, and he gave the poor fisherman half his lands. And they were married and lived happily forever.

It wasn't really a very good story. It borrowed a lot from other stories. But it told me a lot about poor Anita. It told me why Rafael suddenly decided to work in the port for six months. It told me why he brought her a gold ring in the shape of a fish.

I went back to my uncle's house. It was late at night, but I sat with him and drank coffee. My head was full of changing ideas. I said very little, but I thought a lot.

'Have you learned anything important or useful?' asked my uncle.

'I don't know,' I said. 'I can't tell you what Marta told me. I promised to keep it a secret. But are you sure about what you told me? You haven't made any mistakes?'

My uncle thought for a few seconds. 'Yes, I'm sure. I haven't forgotten anything important,' he said.

'Did Rafael really come to the café when the soldier was still there? Are you sure about that?'

'Oh yes. I'm sure. I remember how they looked. Rafael was clean and fine in his best clothes. The soldier was sitting at the table with his friends round him. But he was looking at Rafael all the time. They were like two dogs, looking for a fight.'

'And Rafael stayed in the café and danced until late at night. And you were with him all that time.'

'I was with the poor boy all the time until nearly midnight. Then I closed the café and sent him home.'

'Then how did Anita give him the ring?' I asked myself. 'She didn't leave the house until the music was playing in the café. And at that time she had the ring on her hand. And Rafael was already in the café with the soldier. And he stayed there until midnight, about two hours after the soldier left in his boat.'

Chapter 11   Rosa's Promise

That night I slept badly. Poor Rafael with his mad eyes came into my dreams many times. He was holding the gold ring. He was showing it to me and asking me to help him.

The next morning I sat outside my uncle's house. I looked out at the calm blue sea. I was very tired and unhappy. Soon my uncle came out and sat with me. His wife Rosa brought out coffee and eggs for us.

'What will you do now?' asked my uncle.

'I don't know. I still don't know why Rafael went mad. I still don't know when exactly. I can't believe that a man can go crazy for love of a girl. You say Anita was very beautiful. But a strong young man doesn't go mad for love. Rodrigo is right. I can't explain it. But I'm sure it was something more strange, more terrible. There is a reason, but I haven't found it. I think nobody here in the village knows it.'

'So, what will you do?' asked my uncle again.

'I'll take Rafael to the hospital in the capital. If you help me, I'll give him some medicine. Then he'll go to sleep. When he's in hospital, I can begin to help him. I believe something terrible happened to him. I don't mean when Anita ran away with the soldier. I mean something really terrible, something strange and frightening. Rafael is afraid to remember it. That's why he's mad. At the hospital I can give him modern medicines. They'll help him to sleep and to feel happy. Then perhaps he'll remember what happened to him. If he can remember, he'll get better.'

Rosa was standing in the door. She came to me and took my hand. She looked into my face. Her eyes were full of tears and she looked terribly afraid. 'Please don't take Rafael to hospital,' she said. 'Leave him here in the village with us. He'll be all right with us.'

I was surprised. There were tears in her eyes. She really was very worried and afraid. I thought it was the hospital. Village people are often afraid of hospitals. They believe that people only go to hospitals to die.

'Please don't worry, Aunt Rosa,' I said calmly. 'I won't hurt him. I really think I can help him to remember. With God's help, perhaps I can make him better.'

'He mustn't remember,' she cried. 'He's mad because of his crime. He went mad because of the terrible thing that he did. He mustn't remember. If he remembers, he'll die.'

My uncle and I looked at Rosa. We were very surprised. Her face was red and tears were running down her face.

'What do you know about Rafael's madness?' asked my uncle quietly. 'I'm sure you know something. Tell us now.'

Rosa put her wet face in her hands.

'I promised poor Clara not to tell,' she cried. 'I promised her on her death bed. But if you leave her poor son here with us, I'll tell you.'

Rosa dried her eyes. She sat on the steps in front of the house. She didn't look at us. She looked out at the sea all the time as she told her story.

'I sat with his mother, my sister, when she was very ill five years ago. Before she died, I promised to be a mother to her poor, mad son.'

'We know that,' said my uncle. 'You and I agreed to look after him. And we have. But what did she tell you about why Rafael went mad?'

Rosa put her face in her hands.

'Please don't tell anyone,' she cried. 'I promised to keep her secret forever.'

'We promise,' I said. 'What secret?'

'The secret of Rafael's madness,' said Rosa. 'His mother knew it. But she kept his secret from everyone. He was mad because he did a terrible thing. He did it for love, from hate, the poor, poor boy.'

'What did he do?'

'He killed a man. He took another man's life. The worst crime of all. He murdered the soldier, because of his love for Anita.'

'He did what? But that's impossible!' shouted my uncle.

'That's what Clara told me,' said Rosa. 'She told me everything only hours before she died. She couldn't meet God with that secret in her heart.'

'But how? When?' I asked her quietly. 'Did she say?'

'I'll tell you what Clara told me,' said Rosa. 'Her words are written in fire on my heart. I'll never forget them.'

Chapter 12   A Terrible Secret

Told to Rosa by Clara

It happened that Sunday evening (said Clara).

It was the evening before Anita went away. I cooked some fish and rice for myself and Rafael. Soon it was ready, but Rafael was out in his boat. He often went out soon after it was dark. That day he was out for more than an hour.

Then I heard his boat come on to the beach near our house. As you know, the house stands alone at the end of the village. But still Rafael didn't come to the house, and the food was getting cold and dry.

So I took the small oil lamp from my kitchen and I went down to the sea to find him.

The boat was half on the sand and half in the water. Rafael was standing next to it. He was washing the inside of the boat. There was a lot of water in the bottom of it. I came near with the small lamp. The light shone on Rafael and the boat. He was very wet – his head and hair, his clothes. The water was running down him.

Then I saw something terrible. There was blood on Rafael's clothes. Blood in his hair. Blood running down his face. His wet shirt and trousers were covered in it. There was fresh blood on his hands, red in the light of the lamp.

'God save us!' I said. 'What's happened?'

'I'm all right, mother,' he answered. 'Don't be afraid. But I've killed the stranger who came here to steal my true love.'

Then I saw that all the water in the bottom of the boat was dark with blood.

I put out the lamp immediately. There was no moon and the night was dark. I looked round at the empty beach.

'Take off those clothes,' I said quietly. 'Wash yourself in the sea until you're clean. Then go to the house and put on clean clothes. Go quickly to the café, so people can see you. I'll wash your clothes and the boat. Nobody will know what you've done. If the soldier stops coming here, people won't be very surprised. The man was a stranger. He had no family or close friends.'

Rafael did what I told him. He went to the café and stayed there all that evening. While he was there, I washed the boat. Then I washed his shirt and trousers many times, until you couldn't see the blood.

♦

'Oh, Rosa, my dear wife,' said my uncle quietly. 'Have you kept this dark secret in your heart all these years since Clara died?'

'I promised her. She asked me before she died,' cried Rosa.

'She was as mad as her son!' said my uncle angrily. 'We know the soldier ate with Rodrigo in his house that evening. Then he came straight to the café. I saw him and talked to him. He left the café, alive and well, about an hour later. I heard him leave the village in his boat. More important, Rafael was with me in the café when the soldier left. Yes, he was wearing his best clothes and he was very clean. But when Rafael came into the café, the soldier was sitting there, alive. I promise you.'

'Perhaps he followed the soldier in his boat when he left that night. Perhaps he killed him on the sea later,' said Rosa. 'Clara didn't remember the time exactly.'

'Impossible,' said my uncle. 'Rafael stayed in the café with me and a lot of other men. He was dancing to the music. He didn't leave the café for about two hours. And Rafael couldn't catch the soldier's boat. It had an engine. It was a very fast boat.'

'He killed someone,' said Rosa. 'And he *thought* it was the soldier. I don't know who he killed. But that's what his good mother told me. I must believe her. Perhaps Rafael thought he killed the soldier. Then later he saw him in the café and went mad. It was still a terrible crime. Perhaps that's why he went crazy. But who did he kill? No, it's impossible.'

Rosa ran into the house, crying. My uncle and I looked at the empty blue sea. We didn't speak for a long time. There was food on the table, but we didn't feel very hungry.

'Is it possible?' I asked at last.

'What? That Rafael killed somebody by mistake. No. It's not possible.'

'But his mother's story . . .'

'Listen!' said my uncle. 'I'm not stupid. When Rafael came into the café, he saw the soldier. He didn't look surprised. He didn't even look angry. They both listened to the music for about an hour. Rafael was happy. He was smiling and dancing.'

'All right,' I said. 'I believe you. I believe everybody. But this mystery is going to make *me* crazy soon.'

Chapter 13   In the Hospital

All that morning my head went round and round. It was all impossible. I took a notebook and wrote some questions in it. I still have that notebook with me. Sometimes, when I start feeling very proud of myself, I read it.

Question 1: Did Rafael kill someone? Is that why he went mad? His mother thought he did. She saw him covered in blood. But who did he kill?
Not the soldier. He left the café when Rafael was still in it with my uncle.

Not Anita. She was with her sister until the music started in the café. And Rafael was inside the café then.

So who?

Impossible!

Question 2: Was the soldier killed, or did he only go away? If he was killed, who killed him?

Not Rafael. He was in the café until midnight.

Not Anita. She was a child, and loved him.

Who could kill him? He was a strong young man, a soldier. And he was friendly with everyone in the village.

Impossible!

Question 3: Did Anita run away with the soldier, or was she killed, too? If she was killed, who killed her?

Not Rafael. He loved her. And he was in the café all evening. Perhaps the soldier, and he then ran away. But why? He loved her and wanted to marry her.

And if the soldier killed her, why did Rafael go mad?

Impossible!

I read all my notes and questions again and again. Everything seemed impossible.

Suddenly I looked at them again. There was someone in the village who was big enough and strong enough. Someone who could kill the soldier. He had a good reason to kill him. There was someone who had a good reason to kill Anita, too. Perhaps he saw her leaving the house with her bag that night. Perhaps he followed her along the dark and empty beach, quietly through the soft sand. Perhaps he saw her meet the soldier. Perhaps he killed both of them and put their dead bodies deep in the sea.

There *was* another man who loved Anita. And that man could kill her for running away. He was big enough and strong enough to kill the soldier. That man was Rodrigo, her father.

But then *the wrong man was mad.*

♦

I am a doctor, not a policeman or a detective. I believed I was a clever man, more intelligent than the people of the village. I was too proud of myself. I told my uncle and all the people of the village about my plans to help poor Rafael. I, the great doctor from the university in the city, could make him well again.

I was too proud. I spent a week in the village and I talked to a lot of people. But I still knew nothing about Rafael's madness. I still had no idea what happened to the soldier or Anita. I couldn't be sure that Rodrigo killed them. It was a stupid idea. I didn't really believe it.

I promised Rosa and Marta to tell nobody what they told me. It was our secret. I went back to my hospital to do my work. I wasn't so proud. I decided not to think about what happened in the village. It wasn't a good idea to try to change things.

♦

I heard nothing from my uncle or anyone in the village for almost a year. I often dreamt of Rafael and his gold ring when I was very tired. But I never went back to the village. I didn't want to meet those good people. I was sure they didn't have a good opinion of me now.

Then, one day, a fisherman brought a note to the hospital. It was written by Rodrigo, the shopkeeper. It said:

Rafael is very ill. We think he's dying. Please come immediately. Only you can help us. Please come. Remember my dear daughter Anita and poor, mad Rafael and help us. Your uncle asked me to write this letter. But I want you to come, too. Perhaps at last we can find out what really happened to my daughter all those many years ago.

Rodrigo García

I took a small ambulance from the hospital and went to the village. I was there in a few hours. I went straight to my uncle's house. Rafael was there, lying on a bed. Rosa was putting cold wet cloths on his head. Rafael was very thin and yellow. When I came into the room, he coughed weakly. Blood ran from his mouth. Rosa washed away the blood with another cloth. It was already red with Rafael's blood.

'It's tuberculosis,' I said immediately. 'He's very ill.'

'Yes, I know,' said my uncle. 'That's why I asked you to come. It's very bad. I don't think there's any hope for him.'

'I'll take him to the hospital,' I said. 'I've got an ambulance with me. With medicines and nursing, perhaps we can still save him. But there's not much hope for him. He's very weak.'

We put Rafael in the ambulance and I took him back to the hospital in the city. He was almost dead. We washed him and cut his hair and beard. We put him in a clean bed and gave him medicines.

I sat by his bed for eight hours. He didn't move. He lay like a dead man. His body temperature was very high. Then, very slowly, it began to fall, and he fell into a quiet sleep.

Two days later, he opened his eyes. He was still having medicines and he was very weak. He lay without moving. Only his eyes moved. He looked round the strange white walls, at the plastic bottle above his head. He looked at me in my white coat at his side.

'Am I dead?' he asked, very quietly.

'No, Rafael,' I said. 'You're in hospital. I'm a doctor. Miguel, the owner of the café in your village, is my uncle. Don't be afraid. We're trying to make you well again.'

His mouth moved in a tired smile, and he fell asleep again. I brought a nurse to sit by his bed.

'Tell me if he wakes up. Or if he gets worse,' I said.

Then I went to my room in the hospital and fell on the bed. I was asleep in a few seconds.

There was little hope for poor Rafael. He was thin and weak after all the years that he lived on the beach. For years he ate very little. He slept on the cold, hard ground. The tuberculosis was very bad. He was very, very ill.

But he wasn't mad.

He could speak very little. Most of the time he was very tired. But when he spoke to me, his words were clear and calm. He lived for six days in the hospital. He slept, he woke. And when he was awake, he talked to me. Coughing blood, he told me everything. Then, on the sixth day, he fell quietly asleep. And after a few hours his heart stopped and he was dead. After his long

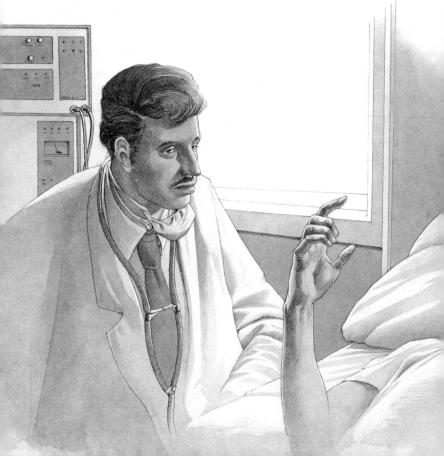

years of pain and madness, I was happy that his death was quiet and easy at the end. He did a terrible thing, a terrible crime. But he paid for it with long years of madness.

I have written his story down here. One day, perhaps, people will read it. But not until all the people in it are dead. Until that day, it must stay a secret.

Chapter 14   The Murder

This is what Rafael told me:

Rafael always loved Anita. He couldn't remember a time when he didn't. It was a small village and the children always played on the beach. Anita and the other girls watched the fishermen. The men cleaned their boats and mended their nets. Rafael fell in love with Anita when they were still children. He loved her, and she loved him. Or she always said so.

But her father wanted her to marry a rich man. A fat old man, perhaps, old and ugly. But he must be rich and important. Rafael could do nothing to change Rodrigo's plans.

There was a place in the rocks at the end of the beach to the west. The children often played in it. It was like a little house in the rocks. In the evenings, Rafael sometimes met Anita there.

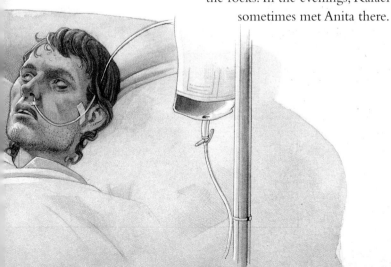

She came out of her house very quietly and ran to their secret place in the rocks. There she and Rafael talked for a few golden minutes. Then she ran home again, afraid of her father. Anita was only fifteen years old at that time. But her head was full of the stories in her books. She was sure she was in love with the handsome young fisherman.

Rafael brought her the gold ring. It was like the magic ring in her story. Her father didn't accept it from Rafael. But Rafael gave it to Anita in secret, when they met later in their secret place in the rocks. The ring was the promise of their love. She wore it when she was with him. At other times she kept it in her room, in the secret place under the carpet.

But then the soldier came to the village. He was an older man. With his bright eyes, his long hair, his boat with an engine, he was much more exciting than Rafael. When he talked with Rodrigo about his life and his travels, Anita heard his stories through the wall of her room. These stories were more exciting than magic lamps and talking fish.

Anita soon thought Rafael was very boring. She stopped meeting him. She stopped speaking to him. Now she was sure she was falling in love with the soldier. But she still kept Rafael's ring, of course.

Rafael was very sad. He wanted the soldier to leave the village and go away for ever. He wanted Anita to come back to him.

But then, one night, Rafael was coming back late from a fishing trip. He saw Anita running along the beach in the moonlight. He watched quietly from the sea. He saw Anita meet the soldier in the little house in the rocks. How did the soldier speak to her? How did Anita give him the time and place to meet? Rafael didn't know. Perhaps the soldier gave her a secret note. Perhaps Anita gave him one. They could both read and write.

Rafael left his boat and swam to the shore. He moved very

44

quietly through the rocks. The soldier's boat was in a small piece of open water on the other side of the rocks. It was only about ten minutes from the village along the coast.

Rafael watched and waited until he saw Anita run back to the village. Then he watched the soldier swim back to his boat. After a few minutes, the soldier started his engine and went away to the west. Rafael was very angry. But he was angry with the soldier, not Anita. He hated this man who was a stranger in the village. A man who the people all accepted as a friend. But a man who was now stealing Anita, his own true love, from them.

Next time the soldier came to the village, Rafael watched him. When the soldier went away in the evening, Rafael went quietly along the beach to the place in the rocks. Soon the soldier's boat came back into the place in the rocks and he lowered his anchor. The soldier swam for a few minutes in the moonlight. Then he sat in the boat again and smoked a cigarette.

He sat for a long time, looking sometimes at his watch. At last he swam to the beach and went to the secret place in the rocks. He waited there. Soon Anita came, hurrying over the rocks. She and the soldier kissed. Long, loving kisses. They sat in the little house in the rocks. The soldier held her close. They talked and laughed and kissed again. And all the time Rafael watched and listened to them with black hate in his heart.

After that, Rafael followed the soldier every time he came to the village. The soldier did the same every time. Sometimes Anita didn't come to the place in the rocks. But the soldier always waited for her there.

Then Rafael knew how to kill the soldier. It was a good plan.

The next time the soldier came to the village, Rafael's plan was ready. The soldier arrived in the village that Sunday and went to Rodrigo's shop with the tin of paraffin. Rafael waited until it was dark. He saw the bright light of the lamp in Rodrigo's house. He watched the soldier start to eat the meal with Rodrigo.

45

He had everything that he needed in his boat. He sailed out quietly to the place in the rocks. The place where the soldier always waited. He took his boat close to the shore and tied it to a rock. Then he went on foot to old Santiago's farm. The old donkey was standing sleeping in its field. Rafael walked with it down to the beach near his boat. It wasn't very far. There he took the old donkey into the water, and then killed it.

He put the dead animal into his boat and went out into deeper water. He went to the place where the soldier usually left his boat. There he began to cut up the dead donkey, throwing the pieces into the sea. He and the boat were soon covered in the donkey's blood. But there was much more blood in the water all round the boat. Rafael knew that the sharks, far away in the sea, could smell it.

Rafael kept the back legs of the donkey in his boat. He took a long, strong piece of line and tied the legs to it. Then he sailed quietly back to the village. There was no moon that night, only the light from the stars. Soon he could see the beach and the houses of the village. The lamp was still burning in Rodrigo's house. The soldier's boat was a few metres from the shore. It was always in the same place. The soldier didn't want to break his engine.

Rafael moved his boat close to the soldier's boat and stopped. He went into the dark water and swam across to it. He had the end of the line in his teeth. He tied it to the bottom of the soldier's boat. Then he swam back to his boat and put the legs of the donkey quietly into the water. Now, the soldier's boat had the smell of blood behind it.

Rafael took his boat to the far end of the beach in front of his house. He pulled it half on to the sand, and began to wash the donkey's blood from the bottom of the boat. He washed some of the blood from his clothes in the sea. But there was a lot of blood and water in the boat.

Suddenly his mother came with an oil lamp. She saw the blood on his clothes and in the boat. She was afraid he was hurt.

'Don't be afraid, mother,' he said. 'I'm not hurt. This isn't my blood. I've killed the soldier.'

It was true. The soldier wasn't yet dead, but Rafael's plans were made.

Rafael wasn't afraid to tell his mother. She always kept his secrets. She was very calm when he told her. She sent him to the house to change his clothes. She stayed and cleaned the boat.

When he went to the café, he found the soldier there. He was surprised. He thought the soldier was spending the evening with Rodrigo. Rafael looked at the soldier, his enemy. He was smiling and laughing with his friends. Rafael thought, 'The sharks are already waiting for you. Tonight you're going to your death.'

The soldier left in the middle of the evening. He went out to his boat, started the engine and went off to the west.

Rafael stayed in the café, listening to the music. He was afraid, but he was excited, too. When he heard the music, he began to dance to the songs. Eyes closed, he saw in his head the soldier's boat. It went through the dark night. Behind it, the red line of blood, dark in the water. The engine stopped. The boat came quietly back to the secret place in the rocks. The soldier waited in the moonlight, smoking a cigarette. Perhaps, then, he jumped into the dark sea for a swim. Something was waiting there, something big and hungry. It moved fast through the water. Perhaps there was time for one short scream. Then all was quiet again. The dark waters were calm. And the soldier was gone for ever.

Rafael danced and smiled and saw these pictures again and again. He stayed and danced until midnight.

Then he went back to his house and went to bed. But he slept only for a few hours. Before the first light of day, he got up quietly and went out of the house. He took his boat along the coast to find the soldier's boat.

The boat was there in the place in the rocks. It lay empty and quiet in the water. Rafael looked for the soldier in the sea and on the land. But there was no sign of him. Nothing was left of him. Rafael saw the long shadows of sharks still swimming in the water near the boat. The boat's engine was above the water. There was a long piece of fishing line tied many times round it.

Rafael laughed.

'My plan was better than I thought,' he said to himself. 'I tied the legs of the old donkey to his boat with some fishing line. And the line also stopped the engine. So the soldier had to go into the water to untie it.'

Rafael took the soldier's boat far from the shore. There he made a hole in the bottom and pushed it under the water. Soon it went down to the bottom of the sea.

Rafael was happy. The soldier and his boat were at the bottom of the sea. Nobody knew what happened to him. He went back to the village and into the house to have an early breakfast. Suddenly he was very hungry.

Chapter 15   The Truth, at Last

A little later (Rafael told me), he and his mother heard the shouting and screaming from Rodrigo's house. They soon learned that Anita was nowhere in the house or the village. Rafael smiled to himself. Perhaps Anita was still waiting somewhere for her soldier. 'She can wait forever. She'll never see him again,' he thought.

'I'll sail along the coast and look for her,' he told his mother. In fact, he wanted to go to a quiet place to wash his boat again. There was still some dark blood in the bottom.

He went back to the place in the rocks.

48

It was calm and quiet there. The soldier's boat was at the bottom of the sea. Rafael took some water from the sea to wash his boat. A small shark swam slowly under it. Almost without thinking, Rafael picked up his fishing spear. He hit the shark hard through the back of the head. Its blood came out into the clear water. A few other sharks, bigger ones, smelt the blood and came fast through the water. They began to bite at the dying fish with their great, sharp teeth. They fought, biting great pieces off the dead shark.

Rafael decided to catch one or two and cut them up in his boat. He wanted their blood to be in the boat with the donkey's.

A white shark about three metres long was pulling at the dead one. It lay in the water next to the boat, not moving. Rafael killed it with his spear and put a line round its head. Then he pulled it into the bottom of the boat.

Rafael took his knife and cut the shark open from neck to tail. Pieces of meat, fish and hair from its stomach fell out into the bottom of the boat. There was a large piece of donkey skin with its grey hair. Rafael moved it with his knife.

In that second, the world stopped. Rafael's blood seemed to freeze inside him. The sky went dark. He couldn't move.

In the pile of meat and fish in the bottom of the boat there was a hand. A complete hand, white and clean.

It was cut off at the wrist with one clean bite. It was a small hand, with small, pretty fingers. The fingernails were long and pink. They weren't bitten or dirty or broken by housework.

And on the middle finger of the hand was a gold ring, a ring in the shape of a golden fish.

Rafael gave one great scream. He held his head in his hands. He knew now where Anita was. The night before, when the engine of the soldier's boat stopped working, she was there in the boat with him. Then he went into the water to look at the engine. She stayed in the boat. She saw him, when the sharks killed him in the dark water. Perhaps she tried to pull him into the boat. But then she too fell into the blood-red water. And there she spent the last terrible seconds of her life with her true prince, the soldier.

Rafael knew he couldn't continue living. He couldn't live with this terrible secret. He stood up in the boat and called Anita's name. Then he threw himself into the sea. He lay in the water, face down. He waited for the sharp teeth in the mouths of the sharks to pull him down to his death. But they didn't. He felt them in the water all round him. Sometimes he felt them push against him. But they didn't hurt him.

Then Rafael understood. God didn't want him to die this way. An easy death. A quick death. Too quick and easy for a murderer. He was terribly afraid. He tried to kill himself. He held his face under the water and tried to die. But he couldn't.

At last he climbed back into the boat. He sat like a dead man and looked at the little hand with the gold ring. After a long time he took the ring carefully from her finger. He took a piece of fishing line and tied the ring round his neck. He had his ring again. He had it from Anita's own hand. 'I'll keep it with me forever,' he thought. 'Then I will never forget my terrible crime.'

He threw the dead shark back into the sea.

Then, last of all, he took the cold white hand. He held it in his own hand for the last time. Then he put it carefully into the water.

Then he lay down in the bottom of the boat holding the ring at his neck. And he looked at the bright sky and talked to Anita. And they laughed and laughed . . .

♦

I took Rafael's body back to his village. He lies in the ground near that place in the rocks. The secret place where he and Anita spent many happy hours. I put the gold ring round his neck. The ring that he took from Anita's dead hand. It will stay with him forever.

Nobody in the village knows what he did. Not Rodrigo, not my uncle or Rosa. They still believe that Anita and the soldier are living somewhere far away.

I can see no reason to tell them anything different.

ACTIVITIES

Chapters 1–4

Before you read

1 This story is called *The Ring*. Who wears rings? Why are they often very important?

2 Which is the right word to end these sentences? Find the words in *italics* in your dictionary. They are all in the story.

   a A *mad* man is always   dangerous/crazy/clever.

   b A *shark* lives in the   sea/forest/mountains.

   c You use a *lamp* when it is   raining/cold/dark.

   d The *shore* is the land next to   a garden/the sea/a wood.

   e *Paraffin* is used in   cars/lamps/toys.

   f *Batteries* are used in   radios/books/pens.

3 Find these words in your dictionary. They are all things that a fisherman uses.

   anchor   engine   net   spear

   Which of them:

   a is long and sharp?

   b makes a boat move through the water?

   c can you use to catch a lot of fish?

   d stops a boat moving?

After you read

4 Answer these questions about the story.

   a What happened to Rafael's father? How did this change Rafael's life?

   b How was Anita different from the other girls in the village?

   c How was the soldier different from the other men in the village?

   d Why couldn't Rafael marry Anita?

5 Discuss this question: Do you think Anita fell in love with the soldier? Why (not)?

Chapters 5–12

Before you read

6 Anita and the soldier disappeared late one Saturday night. The next day, Rafael was mad. What do you think happened that night?

7 Find these words in your dictionary. Then read the sentences below. Which are they describing?

carpet   donkey   fingernail   God   goldsmith   load   magic

a He makes beautiful things from gold.
b It is grey with four legs, big ears and a loud voice.
c People use this in stories to do impossible things.
d You have them on your hands.
e You do this when you want to fill a vehicle.
f It lies on the floor and you walk on it.
g Christians talk to Him in church.

After you read

8 Discuss these questions: Why is the gold ring important in the story? Where did it come from? Where is it now?

9 Who says these words? Why are they surprising?

a 'I don't have a daughter called Anita. I had one many years ago, but she's dead.'
b 'She had many strange and silly ideas in her head.'
c 'I've killed the stranger who came here to steal my true love.'

Chapters 13–15

Before you read

10 Discuss these questions:

a Do you know what made Rafael mad? What do you think happened to Anita and the soldier?
b Before the end of the book, the doctor finds out what really happened that night. Who tells him, do you think?

11 What are these sentences in your language? Find the words in *italics* in your dictionary.

    a She died of *tuberculosis*.

    b He travelled to hospital in an *ambulance*.

    c Please tell me the *truth*.

After you read

12 Answer these questions.

    a When and why exactly did Rafael go mad?

    b How did Anita give the gold ring back to Rafael?

13 Work with another student. Imagine that, one day, the doctor meets the old goldsmith.

    Student A: You are the doctor. Tell the goldsmith why Rafael wanted the ring. Tell him what happened to it later.

    Student B: You are the goldsmith. Ask questions about this strange story.

Writing

14 This book is a story of death and madness. Who dies? How? Who goes mad? Why?

15 *The Ring* is also a love story. Describe the different kinds of love that we read about.

16 Which of these people are 'good' or 'bad'? Why? Write about your opinions.

    the doctor   the soldier   Anita   Aunt Rosa   Rafael

17 Write your own short story about a ring.

Answers for the Activities in this book are available from your local office or alternatively write to: Penguin Readers Marketing Department, Pearson Education, Edinburgh Gate, Harlow, Essex CM20 2JE.